RESPONSE AGAINST ARIANS

St. Fulgentius
Bishop of Ruspe

Translated by: D.P. Curtin

Copyright @ 2024 Dalcassian Press LLC

All rights reserved. No part of this publication may be reproduced, distributed, or transmitted in any form or by any means, including photocopying, recording, or other electronic or mechanical methods, without the prior written permission of the publisher, except in the case of brief quotations embodied in critical reviews and certain other non-commercial uses permitted by copyright law. For permission request, write to Dalcassian Press LLC at dalcassianpublishing at gmail.com

ISBN: 979-8-8693-5500-3 (Paperback)

Library of Congress Control Number:
Author: Curtin, D.P. (1985-)

Printed by Ingram Content Group, 1 Ingram Blvd, La Vergne, Tennessee

First printing edition 2024.

RESPONSE AGAINST ARIANS

For the Catholic faith

1. That the most reliable foundation of the Catholic faith is the apostles after Christ, the sure integrity of the faith testifies: what reason, perhaps the preaching itself has ceased, I do not know what secret operation of the Holy Spirit sown and concreted in the minds of the faithful insinuates. But who is ignorant of those who believe well that all heretics have come out of Catholicism, like useless branches thrown from the vine? But she remains in her root, in her vine, in her love, and the gates of hell will not prevail against her (Matt. 16:18). The one Church, the true Church, the Catholic Church, fighting against all heresies, can fight, cannot be attacked: of which Solomon, in the Song of Songs, in the person of Christ, praising his bride, whom we believe is the Church, says: Behold, my neighbor is like a lily in the midst of thorns (Song 2:2): because his integrity is pricked like thorns every day by the dogmas of different heresies, so that he may be exercised in vigilance against his enemies, until he stands out like a lily on the head of his bridegroom and is adorned with the very whiteness.

2. It is true that some, acting in their own spirit, assumed that the worshipers of his faith should be called Homousians or Unisubstantians, to answer for his inexperience. For so great and such is the almighty God, that he can pronounce good things through evil; as through the evil pontiff (John 11:49), he deigned to foretell the sacrament of our redemption. For he who himself founded the book conceived in a savage mind, thought that the accumulation of divine testimonies, both of the New and of the Old Testament, was opposed to homousion. The Apostle once foretold about such, saying: Not knowing of whom they speak, nor of whom they affirm (1 Tim. 1:7). For if he knew what homousion is expressed in Latin from the Greek, he would strive to praise rather than reproach. For our three hundred and eighteen fathers, who devised the antidote of this word to exclude the poisons of Arius, did not use foreign words from the Gospel, but took care to insinuate the reason of the right faith to those who were not yet intelligent, more easily from word to word. For men are called one, the substance of which is used in the Greek language. Consult the words of the Gospel, and you will find that this was uttered by the mouth of God, I and the Father are one (John 10:30). Discuss the plural and return to the singular truth of substance. For when he said, I and the Father are one, he promulgated the opinion of the Father and his own person, against Sabellius, who foresaw the heretic's future, saying that we are, so that he might distinguish between his own and the Father's person. One thing that he said, he equally foresaw Arius, who did not hesitate to intersect the substance of the deity. Because both Sabellius had joined together badly, and Arius had more wickedly separated them. For it was necessary for Sabellius to separate the person of the Father and the Son, and to completely separate the substance of the Arius deity into nothing. Indeed, they think that a great crime of faith is applied to the Catholics, when they call their disciples Homousians or Unisubstantians; just as the authors of different heresies felt that a sect of their own name should be preached to the disciples. As the Simonians from Simon, the Menandrians from Menander, the Marcionists from Marcion, the Valentinianists from Valens, the Manichaeans from Man, the Nepotians from Nepotus; and in order to pass over the ancient and almost defunct heresies, I will in the meantime mention the new ones: as the Sabellians from Sabellius, the Arians from Arius, the Eunomians from Eunomius, the Macedonians from Macedonius, the Apollinarists from Apollinare, the Nestorians from Nestorius, the Donatists from Donatus, the Maximianists from Maximian, the Rogatists from By request; and if there are others who hold only in name, they are called

Christians, not in deed, who, forsaking God, worship the names of their authors. Let him who thought to accuse Catholics of homousion teach that the name of any man is homousion. For it seemed to me that, unless the most glorious summit of the Gospel had been made more clearly known to all the nations, so that the Arians thought how to foster their heresy, they could have eradicated the very words of the Lord from the Gospel; that is, I and the Father are one: which (as has been said) translated word from word, the Fathers established homousion.

3. But what they devise among the uninitiated, is it to be believed by many, or by a few; I will summarize the fact that the Council of Nicaea was celebrated in three hundred and eighteen Fathers, but that of Ariminense was assembled in eight hundred and thirty, where clever men tried to interpolate homousion among the ignorant. Behold, he obtained homousion in a few, so that he became known to the other bishops appointed throughout the whole world, so that they rejoiced to be decorated with his confession. But if the latter of Ariminensis (it seems that the meeting is lacking) had gathered in such a large number, as they assert, his sect of bishops would be multiplied throughout the world, the people would increase, such a faith would even occupy the empires themselves. But when the cunning of that fraud was recognized by the most prudent and trustworthy men, the homousion was so confirmed, that we see that scarcely a remnant of Arians remained to prove the Catholics. Let us consult the city of Ariminum itself, where this business of fraud was carried out, or rather, if it pleases, was prepared. I do not know whether he has a bishop of his own sect: for I speak more freely of Milan, where Auxentius poured out the poisons of his sect like a cunning artificer; and its term is considered as a kind of contagion. By whom the faith of Ambrose and Augustus was then confirmed to Gratian, and the affections of the bishops and the people grew more and more. For God is not omnipotent; who, through all the Scriptures of his Church, has promised to leave his promise, and to let falsity grow.

Let this be said of all heresies.

4. Moreover, in the consequences, adjuvant to God, who both instructs the heart and rules the tongue, and of one God, and of power, and invisibility, or

the equality of the Son with the Father, and the deity of the Holy Spirit, which Trinity, to those who do not want it, yet is one. God, such evidence may be set forth, that if they did not love the darkness of strife, they must see the light of truth. And let no one be moved by what we have said, that the cremation of the Church was promised throughout all the Scriptures, and if they claim that it was granted through this oppression, let them know that it is written in Jeremiah: The partridge will cry, he will gather those he did not bear, he will make his riches not with judgment (Jer. 17:11). And this is the most certain proof that the Catholic faith never grew except through tribulations and persecutions: so that what was said may be fulfilled, because through many tribulations and distresses we must see the kingdom of God (Acts 14:21). And the exiles of the innocent, and the proscriptions of the miserable, and the torments and oppression of the captives testify to the cremation of his faith. But I see that some contradictors are giving birth, and are accusing us of the persecutions of the Donatists, whose fury has done violence to the laws, and they have suffered by these laws. For if the Catholic mother received those of them in her pious bosom, without any injury of baptism, without any loss of burden, without any insult to the Holy Spirit: so that those who were converted by will may grieve because charity had long hid them.

Catholic testimonies about one God.

5. The first voice of God, Hear, Israel, the Lord your God, God is one (Deut. 6:4). In Deuteronomy, the Lord alone led them, and there was no foreign God with them (Deut. 32:12). Also there, See, see that I am God, and there is no other besides me (Deut. 32:39). Also in Exodus, you shall have no other gods besides me (Exodus 20:3). Also, sacrificing to other gods besides me will be eradicated (Deut. 32:5.) Also, you shall worship the Lord your God and serve him alone (Deut. 6:13). Likewise, for there is no other God, either in heaven or on earth, who can do your works, or be compared to your greatness (Deut. 3:24). In the prophet Hosea, you do not know the Lord apart from me, and there will be no savior apart from me (Hos. 13:4). In Isaiah, I am God, and there is none who saves besides me: I have announced, and I have saved, and there shall be no stranger among you (Is. 43:11). Who above, These things says the Lord, who made the heavens; this God who stretched out the earth and made it: he did not make it in vain, but to be inhabited. I am, I am, and there is

no one else. I am God, and there is no other (Is. 45:18). I swear by myself, unless righteousness proceeds from my mouth, my words will not return for to me every knee will bow, and every tongue will swear to God (Is. 45:22-24). Those above, From the beginning we have not heard, nor have our eyes seen God apart from you (Is. 64:4); and, before me there was no God, and besides me there will be no other (Isa. 43:10). I am the first God, and I am in the things that are to come (Is. 44:6). In the body of the Psalms, who is God but our Lord (Ps. 17:32)? Also, who is a great God like our God? You are God who alone does wonders (Ps. 76:15). Also, Let the nations know that your name is Lord: you alone are the highest above all the earth (Ps. 82:16). This belongs more to the Son. In Kingdoms, Hezekiah against Sennacherib, Lord God of Israel, you are the only God of all the kings of the earth (4 Ki. 19:15). Who above, Lord our God, save us from their hand: that all the kingdoms of the earth may know that you are the only Lord (4 Ki.19:19). Solomon in prayer spread his hands to heaven and said: Lord God of Israel, there is no God like you, neither in heaven above, nor on earth below (3 Ki. 8:23). And although two or three testimonies of one God are sufficient, let those who introduce two gods to us listen. For they confess God the Father and God the Son: this is of course true; but he who does not honor the Son as he honors the Father is impious. For if sacrifice or honor is due to the Father, this is also due to the Son. But when you assert that the Father is greater and the Son less, you introduce two gods: in both you are blasphemous, and by not hearing, The Lord your God, God is one (Deut. 6:4), and not by honoring the Son as you honor the Father. The Son did not take any steps. Ask the Father what is the honor. You are trying to insult both, and the Father, because his Son is not heard, of whom the Father says, Listen to Him (Matt. 17:5), and the Son, whom you dare to despise in his commandment. But now other proofs of the equality of the Father and the Son are put forward.

Testimony of the equality of the Father and the Son.

6. In the Apocalypse, and he had on his garment, or on his thigh, written, King of kings, and Lord of lords (Rev. 19:16; 1 Tim. 6:15). If the Apostle says this about the Father, it is clearly said about the Son. Where above, Blessed and holy is he who has a part in the first resurrection. The second death has no power over them: but they will be priests of God and of his Christ, and they will reign

with him (Rev. 20:6). Where above, I am α and ω, the beginning and the end. I will give to the thirsty the fountain of the water of life for free. He who overcomes will possess these things, and I will be his God, and he will be my son (Rev. 21:6). Where above, And I did not see a temple in it. For the Lord God Almighty is his temple, and the Lamb (Rev. 21:22). No difference. Where above, And he showed me a splendid river of the water of life, proceeding from the seat of God and of the Lamb (Rev. 22:1). One seat, not two. Where above, the Seats of God and the Lamb will be there, and they will serve him (Rev. 21:3). In the Epistle of John, everyone who does not abide in the doctrine of Christ does not have God. He who perseveres in doctrine has both the Son and the Father (2 John, 9). Son first. In the Epistle of Jude, denying our Lord and God Jesus Christ (Jude 4). And God, and the Lord. In the Apocalypse, they say to the mountains and rocks, hide us from the face of Him who sits on the throne, and from the wrath of the Lamb: for the great day of their wrath is coming, and who will be able to stand (Rev. 6:16)? One or equal judgement. Where above, Salvation to our God and to the Lamb (Rev. 7:10). Where above, the kingdom of this world has been made, of the Lord our God, and of his Christ, and it will reign for ever and ever (Rev. 11:15). He will reign, they will not reign. Where above, And I heard a great voice in heaven saying, Salvation, and power, and the kingdom of our God, and the power of his Christ have been accomplished (Rev. 12:10). No division. Where above, And I looked, and behold, the Lamb was standing on Mount Zion, and with him a hundred and forty-four thousand, having his name and the name of his Father written on their foreheads (Rev. 14:1). Does it prejudge, because the Son is named first, where there is one power? Where above, these were bought from men, the firstfruits to God and to the Lamb (Rev. 14:4). Where above, these shall fight with the Lamb, and the Lamb shall overcome them: for he is Lord of lords, and King of kings (Rev. 17:14). What more does the Father have? It is said To the Hebrews, when God promised to Abraham, because he had no one by whom he could swear a greater oath, he swore by himself, saying (Heb. 6:13). If it is received from the Father, it will be visible; if of the Son, he will not be greater than that. Father in the Gospel, that all may honor the Son as they honor the Father (John 5:23). And since he has one who sent him, this mission is not from place to place. For the sun also sends out rays and is not separated from itself. Likewise, as the Father quickens the dead, so also the Son quickens whom he wills (John 5:21). Behold the Son whom He wills; Behold the Spirit, where he wills. The Son says to Philip: He who sees me sees the Father also (John

14:9). And again: Do you not believe that I am in the Father, and the Father is in me (John 14:11)? Behold the equality of the Father and the Son. Likewise, Father, glorify your Son, that your Son may also glorify you (John 17:1). Equal power. But these are enough concerning the equality of the Son with the Father.

Testimony of the Son's divinity.

7. In Job: He stretches out the heavens alone and walks on the sea as on the earth (Job 9:8). In Jeremiah: This is our God, and no other shall be deputed besides him; who found every way of prudence, and gave it to Jacob his son, and Israel to his beloved. After this he was seen in the lands and conversed with men (Baruch 3:36-38). Is it because the person of the Son is here expressed, by saying, because no other will be deputed apart from him, do we separate the Father from the Godhead? In Isaiah: Egypt is weary, and the business of Ethiopia. Many will come to you and will be your servants; and they will walk behind you, bound in fetters; and they will worship you, and they will supplicate you: because God is in you, and you are God alone, and we did not know: the God of Israel, our Savior (Is. 45:14-15). In this most clear testimony, not only the divinity of the Son, but also the highest equality with the Father is shown. For what he says, God is in you, and you are God, this was said in the Gospel, I am in the Father, and the Father is in me (John 14:11). To the Romans: Whose fathers, and from whom Christ, who is above all God, blessed forever (Rom. 9:5). The proper deities of the Son. To the second Corinthians: Who is the invisible image of God (2 Cor. 4:4). If the image, the truth. Where above: God was in Christ, reconciling the world to himself (II Cor. 5:19). If God is whole, not in part. To the Ephesians: To evangelize the incomprehensible riches of Christ (Eph. 3:8). Is it only Christ's, and not the Father's? To the Colossians: Because in him it pleased him to dwell all the fullness of the divinity bodily (Col. 2:9). Notice here that both all fullness and divinity: where there is nothing to be added. Where above: That God might show among the nations the riches of his sacrament, which is Christ (Col. 1:27). Behold, Christ is the riches of God. Where above: As in the recognition of the sacrament of God, which is Christ: in whom are hidden all the treasures of wisdom and knowledge (Col. 2:3). Complete fullness. To the Philippians: He who was constituted in the form of God (Phil. 2, 6). Do you hear the form,

and deny the equal? Where above: But God the Father himself, and our Lord Jesus Christ direct our way to you (1 Thess. 3, 11). Behold, both direct: equal power. To the first Timothy: That you may keep the unimpeachable command until the coming of our Lord Jesus Christ, whom he will show in his time blessed and only powerful (1 Tim. 6:14), etc. Is it because he said, He alone is powerful, that the Father is excluded from power? To Titus: But the grace of God and of our Savior Jesus Christ has shone upon all men (Tit. 2:11). Where above (Tit. 2:13): Waiting for the blessed hope and the coming of the glory of our great God and Savior Jesus Christ. If God the Son is great, he has nothing less. Where above: But when the kindness and humanity of our Savior Jesus Christ shone forth (Titus 3:4). He neither silenced humanity nor divinity. John to Parthius: That we may believe in his true Son, Jesus Christ. This is the true God and eternal life (1 John 5:20). In this testimony he who denies the perfection of the Son of God is the Antichrist. Second Peter: For in this way the entrance into the eternal kingdom of our Lord and Savior Jesus Christ will be abundantly served to you (2 Pet. 1, 11). And although these few testimonies concerning the divinity of the Son, it is as if a drop had been lifted up from the great sea of the Scriptures themselves: since all the Scriptures bear testimony both to his divinity and also to his humanity as assumed flesh, as he says in the Gospel according to John: Search the Scriptures, because you think in to have eternal life for themselves: and they are they which bear witness of me (John 5:39). He does not say, About us, lest he introduce two gods. In Luke Jesus said to them: These are the words that I spoke to you while I was still with you: because it is necessary to fulfill everything that was written in the law of Moses, and the prophets, and the Psalms, about me (Luke 24:44). Does he exclude the Father from the testimony of the Scriptures, because even here he says, Of me? On the omnipotence of the Son in Solomon: Your word, Lord, is omnipotent; He comes from the heavens from royal seats (Wis. 18:15). In Zechariah: O flee from the land of the north, says the Lord, because I will gather you from the four winds of heaven. Says the Lord: Be saved in Zion who dwells in the daughter of Babylon. For this reason, says the Lord Almighty: After the glory he sent me to the nations that plundered you. Because of this, whoever touches you is like someone who touches the pupil of his eye. Therefore I will bring my hand upon them, and they shall be a prey to those who prey upon them; and you shall know that the Lord Almighty has sent me (Zech. 2:2). The almighty says above, the almighty sends down: are there two almighty? Amos the prophet: The Lord who touches the earth and moves it, and all who dwell in it will mourn; and he shall ascend like the river of Egypt, which builds its ascent upon the heavens, and establishes its release upon the earth: who calls the waters of the sea, and pours them out upon the face of the earth: the Lord Almighty is his name (Amos 9:5). Are not all these things meant to belong to the Son? who, coming down, touched the earth, moved with passion, and ascended from the earth into heaven, and descended from heaven upon the earth, as he himself promised in the Apocalypse (3:14): He who is a faithful witness, the beginning of God's creation, says these things: Who is, and who was, and who is to come, the almighty Lord (Rev. 1:8). It moves, because he said, the beginning of God's creation; move, because it is said, the Lord is omnipotent: as this, of the deity; that which was born of the Virgin Mary.

Evidences of the Trinity

8. In the Gospel: Go, baptize the nations in the name of the Father, and of the Son, and of the Holy Spirit (Matt. 28:19). In the name, not in the names. Also: The kingdom of heaven is like a woman who hid leaven in enough flour for three until it was all fermented (Matt. 13:33). Here the woman is called the Church, which in equal weight hides the faith of the Father, and of the Son, and of the Holy Spirit in the hearts of believers. In the Apocalypse: Holy, holy, holy Lord God of Sabaoth (Rev. 4, 8). Thirdly, I hear the holy and one Lord God. Where above: And the angel said to me: These words are the truth of God. And I fell at his feet to worship him; and he said to me: See that you do not; I am your servant, and of your brothers who have the testimony of Jesus, and the spirit of prophecy (Rev. 19:9-10). What could be more clearly used to show the Trinity than the true words of the Father, the testimony of the Son, the gift of prophecy of the Holy Spirit? In the Psalms: With you is the source of life, and in your light we will see light (Ps. 35:10). Christ is the source of life with God the Father; and because there is light in him, the Holy Spirit is seen as an illuminator: because he who does not have the Spirit of Christ is not his (Rom. 8:9). In Psalm 66:8: May God bless us, our God, may God bless us, and let all the ends of the earth fear him. I hear God three times, and he preaches one thing to be feared. In the Epistle of John: There are three in heaven that bear witness, the Father, the Word, and the Spirit: and the three are one (1 John 5:7). What shall I say of the patriarch Abraham? who, when he saw the appearance of three men, recognized one God in them, when he said: Lord,

Lord (Gen. 18:3). By bodily service to the tribe he presents the duty of humanity; yet he received a boon from one child, while it is said to him: At this time I will come, and he will be the son of Sarah (Gen. 18:10). He did not say we will come, but I will come: lest it should be seen that he should bring in the people of the gods. For in order that you may know that the Trinity dwells at the same time, and at the same time rejects impurity, listen to what the Lord says in the Gospel: He who loves me will be loved by my Father, and I will love him (John 14:21); and, I and my Father will come, and we will make our abode with him (John 14:23). Behold, the Father and the Son dwell in one house. What is the Holy Spirit? Hear the Apostle saying: You are the temple of God, and the Spirit of God dwells in you (1 Cor. 3:16). It is shown that the Father, and the Son, and the Holy Spirit dwell together; it is shown that the Trinity itself declines at the same time from impurity. In Solomon you have: But perverse thoughts separate from God: this of the Father. For wisdom will not enter into a malicious soul: this of the Son. For the Holy Spirit will escape the falsehood of discipline and remove Himself from thoughts which are without understanding (Wis. 1:3, 4:5): this about the Holy Spirit. But as a summary of the understanding, gather the meaning of the Scriptures that speak in unity about the nature of the Trinity, you also have in Exodus: I am the God of Abraham, and the God of Isaac, and the God of Jacob (Ex. 3:6). In the psalm: The Lord lives, and blessed is my God, and may the God of my salvation be exalted (Ps. 17:47). Paul: The same Spirit, the same Lord, the same God (1 Cor. 12:4-6). Does it offend Catholic sense because the Spirit is mentioned first? Likewise, if you seek the Lord, the Trinity itself, listen: Bring to the Lord glory and honor, bring to the Lord glory to his name (Ps. 28:2). Because the King himself is the Trinity: Remove your gates, princes, and lift them up, eternal gates, and the King of glory will enter. Who is this King of glory? The Lord of the virtues is himself the King of glory (Psal. 23:9). Testimony given, God repeated a third time, Lord a third time called a King. Neither gods, nor lords, nor kings are distinguished, because names and persons are distinguished in three: for one deity, one dominion, one royal government. He who contradicts this truth with the desire to overcome evil, I do not say will be damned, but he is already damned.

Evidences of the Holy Spirit, because he is God.

9. At the beginning of the book of Genesis: And the Spirit of God moved upon the waters (Genesis 1:2): who would sanctify the waters in the form of baptism, not who would pause by letting them go. In Job: It is the divine Spirit that made me, and the Spirit of the Almighty that teaches me (Job 33:4). Perfection in the divinity. In the Gospel: God is a spirit, and those who worship him must worship in spirit and in truth (John 4:24). Also: For God does not give the Spirit by measure (John 3:31). Behold, the Spirit is immense. To Nicodemus: For the spirit breathes where it wills, and you hear its voice, and you do not know whence it comes or whither it goes (Ibid., 8). When you hear, Where he wills, it is his own power. Christ in himself: the Spirit of the Lord upon me (Luke 4:18). Unless the intellect recalls these voices piously, the Spirit will be greater than the Son. Also: Jesus, filled with the Holy Spirit, returned from the Jordan (Ibid., 1). A similar understanding. Also: If you then see the Son of man ascending where he was before. It is the spirit that gives life: for the flesh profiteth nothing (John 6:63). He has nothing less than the divinity that gives life. Also: When the Paraclete comes, the Spirit of truth, whom the Father will send in my name, he will introduce you into all truth and teach you (John 16:13). It is God who will introduce into all truth. In the Acts of the Apostles, Peter Cornelius: Jesus of Nazareth, whom God anointed with the Holy Spirit (Acts 10:38). Man is anointed, not God. Also to Ananias: Why did Satan tempt your heart to lie to the Holy Spirit (Acts 5:3)? And he infers: You have not lied to men, but to God (Acts 5: 4). Also: The Holy Spirit says these things: Separate for me Saul and Barnabas, in the ministry to which they are called (Acts 13:2). Here he introduces the person of neither the Father nor the Son, whom, however, the sound understanding does not separate from judgment. Also the Apostle to the Gentiles in his Epistle: It pleased the Holy Spirit and us, he says, to impose no more upon you than to abstain from idols, from fornication, and from blood (Acts 15:28). Was this judgment made without the Father and the Son? Also there: And the Spirit said to Peter: Get up and go with them, because I have sent them to you (Acts 10:19). Does not the Creator command the creatures? Also there: And Paul, sending from Miletus to Ephesus, summoned the presbyters and elders (Acts 20:17); and after much exhortation he brought: Attend to the flock of Christ, in which the Holy Spirit has appointed you bishops (Acts 20:28). Is the Father or the Son separated

from this constitution of the priest? Paul to the Romans: But the Spirit is eternal life and peace (Rom. 8:6). This is the Father, this is the Son, this is the Holy Spirit; but one life, not three. Where above: The Spirit is life because of righteousness (Rom.8:10). This is the Father, this is the Son. Where above: But if the Spirit of him who raised Christ from the dead dwells in you (Rom. 8:11). What kind of God is this who raised the flesh of the Creator from the dead? Where above: For we have not received the spirit of slavery (Rom. 8:15). There is no book but God, who is the Holy Spirit. Where above: May the God of hope fill you with all joy and peace in believing: in the abundance of hope and the power of the Holy Spirit (Rom. 15:13). As Christ is the power of God, so is the Holy Spirit. Where above: That the offering of the Gentiles may be sanctified in the Holy Spirit (Rom. 15:16). As the Spirit quickens, so also sanctifies. Where above: For I do not dare to speak of those things which Christ does not bring about through me into the obedience of the nations, by word and deed; by the power of signs and wonders, in the power of the Holy Spirit (Rom.15:18-19). Power the Son, power the Spirit, power the Father; but one, not three. To the first Corinthians: But the Spirit searcheth all things. No one knows the things of God except his Spirit (1 Cor. 2:10, 11). Where above: You are the temple of God, and the Spirit of God dwells in you (1 Cor. 3:16). It is God who dwells in his temple. Where above: You have been washed and sanctified in the name of our Lord Jesus Christ and in the Spirit of our God (1 Cor. 6:11). Behold, the Son and the Holy Spirit sanctify at the same time. Where above: One and the same Spirit works all things, dividing to each one as he wills (1 Cor. 12:11). He who freely does what he wills is subject to no one. Second to the Corinthians: An epistle written not with ink, but with the Spirit of the living God (II Cor. 3:3). The spirit of man is not inferior to man; how much more the Spirit of God! Where above: The letter kills, but the Spirit gives life (Ibid., 6). He who gives life is God: because the Lord mortifies and gives life (1 Kings 2:6). To the Galatians: That we may receive the blessing of the Spirit through faith (Gal. 3:14). It is God who blesses. Where above: We live by the Spirit, and we walk by the Spirit (Gal. 5:25). He who blesses again, himself gives life as God. Where above: He who sows in the Spirit, from the Spirit will reap eternal life (Gal. 6:8). In these three testimonies to the Galatians, the Spirit both blesses, and quickens, and gives eternal life. To the Ephesians: In whom you have been sealed as believers in the Holy Spirit (Eph. 1:13). We are sealed in the name of the Father, and of the Son, and of the Holy Spirit. Where above: In which you are built into a habitation of God in the Spirit (Eph. 2:22). Also: It was revealed to his holy apostles in the Spirit that the nations are united (Eph. 3:5). One and the same Spirit works all things: he makes heirs. Where above: That he may give you according to the riches of his glory, strength to be strengthened by his Spirit (Eph.2:16). It is not strengthened except by God. Where above: Be anxious to preserve the unity of the Spirit in the bond of peace (Eph. 4:3). Peace Christ Are the two at peace? Where above: And the sword of the Spirit, which is the word of God (Ephesians 6:17). Christ the Word of God; The Holy Spirit is the word of God. Did the two talk? To the Philippians: Even if I am absent, I will hear about you, because you stand in one Spirit (Phil. 1:27), this is in God. To the Thessalonians: God has taken you from the beginning to salvation in the sanctification of the Spirit (II Thess. 2:12). To the first Timothy: Great is the sacrament of piety, which is manifested in the flesh and justified in the Spirit (1 Tim. 3:16). Behold, even the incarnation of Christ is sanctified by the Holy Spirit. To the second Timothy: Keep the good promise of faith, through the Holy Spirit who dwells in us (2 Tim. 1, 11). If God were not a Spirit, the apostle would not have dared to swear by his disciple. Moreover, who dwells in us. To Titus: He saved us by the washing of regeneration, by the Holy Spirit (Tit. 3:5). Peter to the Gentiles: They were announced to you by those who preached the gospel to you, sent by the Holy Spirit from heaven: in whom the angels desire to look (1 Pet. 1, 12). It is God whom the angels desire to see. Where above: Christ died for our sins, the just for the unjust: that he might offer us to God, being mortified in the flesh, but quickened in the Spirit (1 Pet. 3:18). Where above: That indeed they may be judged according to man in the flesh, but live according to God in the Spirit (1 Peter 4:6). Where above: If you reproach in Christ, because the Spirit of the glory of the Lord rests in you (Ibid., 14). The glory of the Father is Christ, the glory of the Holy Spirit. Are there two glories? Peter's Second: Understanding this first, that every prophecy of the Scriptures is not made by the proper interpretation. For prophecy was not sometimes brought forth by human will, but men of God, moved by the Holy Spirit, spoke (II Pet. 1, 0, 21). No one inspires the gift of prophecy but God. John to Parth: By this we know that he abides in us, from the Holy Spirit whom he gave us (1 John 3:24). Where above: Because we abide in him, and he in us; because he gave us of his Spirit (1 John 4:13). He said that what you hear is the operation of virtue, not the separation of the deity. In the Apocalypse: And after three and a half days, the Spirit of life from God entered into them; and they stood upon their feet (Rev. 11:11). That which proceeds from God is God. Where above: Write, Blessed are the dead who die in the Lord. The Spirit already says that they should rest from their labors (Rev. 14:13). The Father did not say, the Son did not say, but the Spirit, who is shown to be God by this decree. To the Hebrews: For if the blood of bulls and goats, sprinkled with the ashes of a calf, sanctifies the defiled for the cleansing of the flesh, how much more the blood of Christ, who through the Holy Spirit offered himself spotless to God (Heb. 9:13, 14)! This testifies to the power of the Holy Spirit, through whom the flesh of Christ is presented immaculate. Where above: He who does the law of Moses in anger, without any mercy, dies with two or three witnesses. ! Behold, what is the revenge for the injuries of the Son and of the Holy Spirit. Where above: God the judge of all, and the Spirit of the just perfected, and the mediator of the New Testament, Jesus Christ (Heb. 12:23). This testimony corresponds to the Trinity, because both the Father, the Son, and the Holy Spirit are named here. Because the Holy Spirit is omnipotent, in Solomon: the Holy Spirit, manifold, subtle, eloquent, secure, undefiled, having all power (Wis. 7:22). And do you deny the Almighty? Because the Holy Spirit is the judge, the Lord says: If I go away, I will send him to you; and when he comes, he himself will convict the world of sin, of righteousness, and of judgment (John 16:7, 8). Do you see the judge who, if it must be said, vindicates the Saviour? And what can I say more about the deity of the Holy Spirit? whom David feared, saying: Whither shall I go, O Lord, from thy Spirit, or whither shall I flee from thy face (Ps. 138:7)? And to conclude, so great and such is the Holy Spirit, that if anyone blasphemes, he will find him not relaxing, neither in this world, nor in the future.

10. It is impossible to express that ineffable substance or nature of the Divinity in human words: inconvertible, unchangeable, impassive, simple, incomposite, indivisible, unapproachable light, inexplicable power, greatness without end, glory unfathomable, goodness concupiscible, beauty inexhaustible, which indeed touches a pure mind and may move the feeling, but it cannot be indicated or explained. Where is the Father, and the Son, and the Holy Spirit, the only nature that is not created, the power of dominion, the goodness of nature. The Father is the beginning of all things, the cause of all things, the root of living things: from whom proceeds the fountain of life, power, and the immutable image of the invisible God, who is the Son begotten of the Father. The word, or living reason; who was always, and was with God, and was God,

not made from the Father before the ages, not afterwards assumed or adopted as a son, not by possession or creation, but the creator and maker of all things: who is all that the Father is; to whom the Father gave all that he has by begetting. And where, therefore, he who gave, gave by begetting; and he who received, received at birth; the needy was not helped, but abundance itself was born. For the one who received cannot be unequal to the one who gave, because he also received this at birth in order to be equal. For he has nothing less from the Father who said: All that the Father has are mine (John 16:15). And because he emptied himself, taking the form of a servant, not losing the form of God, he became obedient in the same form of a servant even to death, and the death of the cross. in which he was diminished a little less by the angels, that he might remain equal in the form of God, because that form is not changeable. He who is in heaven with worldly intellectual spirits in the form of God and equal to God, as God provides an example; that he might give himself the same example, when he returned even after he had fallen, who could not see God because of the impurity of sins and the penalty of mortality: he emptied himself, not by losing his divinity, but by assuming our humanity; and taking the form of a servant, he came to us in this world, who was in this world, because the world was made through him (John 1:10), as an example to those who see God above, an example to those who marvel at man below: an example of the healthy to remain, an example of the weak to recover; He would become an example of the dying not to fear, an example of the dead to rise again: he himself holding the primacy in all things, so that for happiness man had to follow only God, and he could not feel God. in following God made man, he would at the same time follow whom he could feel, and whom he ought to follow. Let us therefore love him and cling to him, with love diffused in our hearts by the Holy Spirit who has been given to us. This Spirit is both life, and life-giving light, and illumination; good, and goodness; The right spirit, the principal spirit, who is the Lord of all; sending apostles, separating ministers for himself, setting up temples for himself, inspiring where he wills, dividing the gifts of the Spirit as he wills. The Spirit of adoption, the Spirit of truth, the Spirit of wisdom and understanding, of knowledge, of counsel, of power, and of the fear of God: by whom the Father is acknowledged, and the Son is glorified. For it is not worthy that either the Son should ever be absent from the Father, or the Spirit from the Son: for the divinity would be defrauded in the greatest measure, and would be led as if inglorious and unworthy, if, as it were, by penance and foreordained counsel, God had reached the fullness of perfection. He who can receive, let him receive (Matt. 19:12): he who cannot yet pray to receive, believe to receive: because it is written: Unless you believe, you will not understand (Isa. 7:9, according to the LXX).

LATIN TEXT

Pro fide Catholica

1. Catholicae fidei fidissimum fundamentum post Christum apostolos esse, certa fidei testatur integritas: quam rationem, ipsa forsitan praedicatione cessante, occulta nescio quae operatio Spiritus sancti in mentibus fidelium seminata atque concreta insinuat. Quis tamen bene credentium ignorat quia haereses omnes de Catholica exierunt, tanquam sarmenta inutilia de vite projecta? Ipsa autem manet in radice sua, in vite sua, in caritate sua, et portae inferorum non praevalebunt adversus eam (Matth. XVI, 18). Ecclesia una, Ecclesia vera, Ecclesia catholica, contra omnes haereses pugnans, pugnare potest, expugnari non potest: de qua Salomon in Canticis canticorum, ex persona Christi suam sponsam, quam Ecclesiam credimus, laudantis, dicit: Ecce proxima mea tanquam lilium in medio spinarum (Cant. II, 2): quia diversarum haeresum dogmatibus ejus integritas tanquam spinis quotidie pungitur, ut contra hostes suos vigilans exerceatur, donec eminens tanquam lilium in capite sponsi sui candore ipso decoretur.

2. Verum quia quidam, proprio spiritu actus, ejus fidei cultores Homousianos vel Unisubstantianos vocandos esse praesumpsit, ejus imperitiae respondendum. Tantus enim ac talis est omnipotens Deus, ut per malos pronuntiet bona; sicut per pontificem malum (Joan. XI, 49), nostrae redemptionis praedicere dignatus est sacramentum. Is namque qui ipsum condidit libellum saeva mente conceptum, congeriem divinorum testimoniorum tam Novi quam Veteris Testamenti contra homousion opponendam putavit. De talibus olim praenuntiavit Apostolus, dicens: Nescientes de quibus loquantur, neque de quibus affirment (I Tim. I, 7). Si enim sciret quid homousion ex Graeco in Latino exprimitur, laudare potius quam exprobrare contenderet. Patres enim nostri trecenti decem et octo, qui ad Arii venena excludenda antidotum hujus vocabuli confecerunt, non extraneis vocibus ab Evangelio usi sunt, sed verbum e verbo ad ritum facilius, rectae fidei rationem nondum intelligentibus insinuare curarunt. Homos namque unus, usia substantia Graeco sermone appellatur. Consule Evangelii dictum, et invenies hoc esse ore divino prolatum, Ego et Pater unum sumus (Joan. X, 30). Discute pluralem, et redi ad singularem substantiae veritatem. Nam quod dixit, Ego et Pater unum sumus, Patris suamque personam, contra Sabellium, quem praevidebat futurum haereticum, dicendo sumus, sententiam promulgavit, ut

discerneret suam Patrisque personam. Unum quod dixit, aeque Arium praevidebat, qui substantiam deitatis intersecare non dubitat. Quia et Sabellius male conjunxit, et Arius sceleratius separavit. Oportebat namque Sabellium Patris Filiique personam secernere, et Arium deitatis substantiam in nullo penitus separare. Magnum sane crimen fidei putant applicari Catholicae, cum ejus alumnos Homousianos vel Unisubstantianos appellant: quasi homousion vel substantiam deitatis vel alicujus hominis vocabulum contineat; sicut diversarum haeresum auctores sui nominis sectam discipulis praedicandam esse senserunt. Sicut Simoniani a Simone, Menandriani a Menandro, Marcionistae a Marcione, Valentinianistae a Valente, Manichaei a Mane, Nepotiani a Nepote; et ut antiquas et pene jam deficientes haereses praetermittam, novellas interim nominabo: ut sunt Sabelliani a Sabellio, Ariani ab Ario, Eunomiani ab Eunomio, Macedoniani a Macedonio, Apollinaristae ab Apollinare, Nestoriani a Nestorio, Donatistae a Donato, Maximianistae a Maximiano, Rogatistae a Rogato; et si qui sunt alii qui nomine tenus tantum, non opere dicuntur Christiani, qui derelicto Deo, auctorum suorum nomina venerantur. Doceat is qui homousion in catholicos accusandum putavit, alicujus esse hominis nomen homousion. Videretur namque mihi, nisi Evangelii clarissimum culmen omnibus gentibus luce clarius innotuisset, ut haeresim suam quomodo fovendam arbitrarentur Ariani, possent ipsa Domini verba de Evangelio eradicare; id est, Ego et Pater unum sumus: quod (ut dictum est) verbum e verbo translatum, homousion Patres statuerunt.

3. Quod autem apud imperitos astruunt, multis debere credi, an paucis; eo quod Nicaenum concilium in trecentis decem et octo Patribus celebratum est, Ariminense vero in octingentis triginta jactitant congregatum, ubi homousion callidi homines apud imperitos interpolare conati sunt, compendio referam. Ecce homousion in paucis obtinuit, ut caeteris episcopis per totius orbis spatia constitutis sic innotuisset, ut ejus se confessione gaudeant decorari. Quod si posterior Ariminensis (Videtur deesse conventus) in tanta multitudine, ut asserunt, congregatus est, ejus sectae episcopi per orbem multiplicarentur, populi crescerent, talis fides etiam ipsa imperia occuparet. Sed ubi fraudis illius calliditas per prudentes et probatissimos viros est agnita, ita homousion confirmatum est, ut vix Ariminensis reliquias ad probandos catholicos remansisse cernamus. Ipsam urbem Ariminum, ubi hoc fraudis negotium gestum est, vel potius concinnatum, si complacet, consulamus. Utrum ipsius

sectae habeat episcopum nescio: nam de Mediolano liberius astruam, ubi Auxentius sectae suae venena ut callidus artifex fudit: cujus posterior Ambrosius dogma ita destruxit, Spiritu sancto repletus, ut nomen ejus post mortem in ipsa urbe a memoria viventium raderetur; et velut quoddam contagium ejus vocabulum habeatur. Per quem Ambrosium et Augusti tunc Gratiani fides firmata est, et crementa in episcopis et populis magis magisque creverunt. Non enim omnipotens Deus; qui per omnes Scripturas Ecclesiae suae crementa promisit, deserere suam pollicitationem, et dimittere posset crescere falsitatem.

Hoc de omnibus haeresibus dictum sit.

4. Caeterum in consequentibus, adjuvante Deo, qui et cor instruit, et linguam regit, et de uno Deo, et de potentia, et invisibilitate, vel aequalitate Filii cum Patre, et Spiritus sancti deitate, quae Trinitas, ipsis nolentibus, unus tamen est Deus, talia testimonia ponentur, ut si contentionis tenebras non amaverint, lucem necesse sit videant veritatis. Et ne quempiam moveat quod diximus, Ecclesiae crementa per omnes Scripturas fuisse promissa, et si vindicant per hanc oppressionem fuisse concessa, noverint esse scriptum in Jeremia: Clamabit perdix, congregabit quos non peperit, faciet divitias suas non cum judicio (Jer. XVII, 11). Et hoc certissimum documentum est quia catholica fides nunquam nisi tribulationibus et persecutionibus crevit: ut impleatur quod dictum est, Quia per multas tribulationes et angustias oportet nos videre regnum Dei (Act. XIV, 21). Illius autem fidei crementa testantur exsilia innocentium, et proscriptiones miserorum, et tormenta et oppressio captivorum. Sed video quosdam contradictores parturientes, et Donatistarum nobis objicere persecutiones, quorum furor legibus violentiam fecit, et legibus ista perpessi sunt. Nam si quos ex eis catholica mater pio sinu suscepit, sine ulla baptismi injuria, sine ulla oneris jactura, sine ulla Spiritus sancti contumelia: ut qui voluntate conversi sunt, dolerent quia diu eos latuit caritas.

Catholica testimonia de uno Deo.

5. Prima vox Dei, Audi, Israel, Dominus Deus tuus, Deus unus est (Deut. VI, 4). In Deuteronomio, Dominus solus deducebat eos, et non fuit cum illis Deus alienus (Deut. XXXII, 12). Item ibi, Videte, videte quia ego sum Deus, et non est alius praeter me (Ibid., 39). In Exodo item, Non erunt tibi dii alii absque me (Exod. XX, 3). Item, Sacrificans diis aliis absque me, eradicabitur (Ibid., 5.) Item, Dominum Deum tuum adorabis, et illi soli servies (Deut. VI, 13). Item, Neque enim est alius Deus vel in coelo vel in terra, qui potest facere opera tua, aut comparari magnitudini tuae (Deut. III, 24). In Osee propheta, Dominum praeter me non noveris, et salvans non erit praeter me (Ose. XIII, 4). In Isaia, Ego Deus, et non est praeter me salvans: annuntiavi, et salvavi, et non erit in vobis alienus (Isa. XLIII, 11). Qui supra, Haec dicit Dominus, qui fecit coelum; hic Deus qui extendit terram, et fecit eam: non in vanum fecit eam, sed ut inhabitaretur. Ego sum, ego sum, et non est alius quis. Ego sum Deus, et non est alius (Isa. XLV, 18). Per meipsum juro, nisi prodierit de ore meo justitia, verba mea non revertentur: quoniam mihi flectetur omne genu, et jurabit omnis lingua Deum (Ibid., 22, 23 et 24). Qui supra, A saeculo non audivimus, neque oculi nostri viderunt Deum praeter te (Isa. LXIV, 4); et, Ante me non fuit Deus, et praeter me non erit alius quis (Isa. XLIII, 10). Ego Deus primus, et ego in ea quae superveniunt (Isa. XLIV, 6). In corpore Psalmorum, Quis Deus praeter Dominum nostrum (Psal. XVII, 32)? Item, Quis Deus magnus sicut Deus noster? Tu es Deus qui facis mirabilia solus (Psal. LXXVI, 15). Item, Sciant gentes quoniam nomen tibi Dominus: tu solus altissimus super omnem terram (Psal. LXXXII, 16). Hoc magis Filio competit. In Regnorum, Ezechias adversus Sennacherib, Domine Deus Israel, tu es Deus solus regum omnium terrae (IV Reg. XIX, 15). Qui supra, Dominus Deus noster, salvos nos fac de manu eorum: ut sciant omnia regna terrae quia tu es Dominus solus (Ibid., 19). Salomon in oratione expandit manus suas in coelum, et ait: Domine Deus Israel, non est similis tibi Deus nec in coelo sursum, neque in terra deorsum (III Reg. VIII, 23). Et quamvis de uno Deo duo vel tria testimonia sufficerent, audiant tamen ii qui nobis duos deos introducunt. Confitentur enim Deum Patrem, et Deum Filium: hoc sane verum est; sed qui non honorificat Filium sicut honorificat Patrem, hic impius est. Si enim debetur sacrificium vel honorificentia Patri, hoc debetur et Filio. At cum majorem asseris Patrem, minorem Filium, duos deos introducis: in utroque sacrilegus, et non audiendo,

Dominus Deus tuus, Deus unus est (Deut. VI, 4), et non honorificando Filium sicut honorificas Patrem. Nullos gradus interposuit Filius. Interroga Patris quae honorificentia. Tu conaris ad utrorumque contumeliam, et Patris, quia ejus Filius non auditur, de quo Pater dicit, Ipsum audite (Matth. XVII, 5), et Filii, quem in suo praecepto audes contemnere. Sed jam alia testimonia de aequalitate Patris et Filii proponantur.

Testimonia de aequalitate Patris et Filii.

6. In Apocalypsi, Et habebat in vestimento, vel in femore suo scriptum, Rex regum, et Dominus dominantium (Apoc. XIX, 16; I Tim. VI, 15). Si de Patre hoc Apostolus dicit, hic manifeste de Filio dicitur. Ubi supra, Beatus et sanctus qui habet partem in resurrectione prima. In eis secunda mors non habet potestatem: sed erunt sacerdotes Dei et Christi ejus, et regnabunt cum eo (Apoc. XX, 6). Ubi supra, Ego sum α et ω, initium et finis. Ego sitienti dabo fontem aquae vitae gratis. Qui vicerit, possidebit haec, et ero illi Deus, et ipse erit mihi filius (Apoc. XXI, 6). Ubi supra, Et templum non vidi in ea. Dominus enim Deus omnipotens est templum ejus, et Agnus (Ibid., 22). Nulla differentia. Ubi supra, Et ostendit mihi fluvium aquae vitae splendidum, procedentem de sede Dei et Agni (Apoc. XXII, 1). Una sedes, non duae. Ubi supra, Sedes Dei et Agni in illa erunt, et servient ei (Ibid., 3). In Epistola Joannis, Omnis qui non manet in doctrina Christi, Deum non habet. Qui permanet in doctrina, et Filium et Patrem habet (II Joan., 9). Filius prius. In Epistola Judae, Dominatorem et Deum nostrum Jesum Christum negantes (Jud., 4). Et Deus, et Dominus. In Apocalypsi, Dicunt montibus et petris, Abscondite nos a facie sedentis in throno, et ab ira Agni: quoniam venit dies magnus irae ipsorum, et quis poterit stare (Apoc. VI, 16)? Unum, vel aequale judicium. Ubi supra, Salus Deo nostro et Agno (Apoc. VII, 10). Ubi supra, Factum est regnum hujus mundi, Domini Dei nostri, et Christi ejus, et regnabit in saecula saeculorum (Apoc. XI, 15). Regnabit, non Regnabunt. Ubi supra, Et audivi vocem magnam in coelo dicentem, Facta est salus, et virtus, et regnum Dei nostri, et potestas Christi ejus (Apoc. XII, 10). Nulla divisio. Ubi supra, Et vidi, et ecce Agnus stabat super montem Sion, et cum illo centum quadraginta quatuor millia, habentes nomen ejus, et nomen Patris ejus scriptum in frontibus suis (Apoc. XIV, 1). Nunquid praejudicat, quia Filius prior nominatus est, ubi una potestas est? Ubi supra, Hi empti sunt ex hominibus,

primitiae Deo et Agno (Ibid., 4). Ubi supra, Hi cum Agno pugnabunt, et Agnus vincet eos: quia Dominus dominorum est, et Rex regum (Apoc. XVII, 14). Quid amplius habet Pater? Dicatur. Ad Hebraeos, Abrahae namque promittens Deus, quia neminem habuit per quem juraret majorem, juravit per semetipsum dicens (Hebr. VI, 13). Si de Patre accipitur, visibilis erit; si de Filio, major illo non erit. Pater in Evangelio, Ut omnes honorificent Filium, sicut honorificant Patrem (Joan. V, 23). Et quia habet qui eum misit, haec missio non de loco in locum. Nam et sol mittit radios, et non a se separatur. Item, Sicut Pater vivificat mortuos, ita et Filius quos vult vivificat (Ibid., 21). Ecce Filius, quos vult; ecce Spiritus, ubi vult. Filius dicit Philippo: Qui me videt, videt et Patrem (Joan. XIV, 9). Et iterum: Non credis quia ego in Patre, et Pater in me est (Joan. XIV, 11)? Ecce aequalitas Patris et Filii. Item, Pater, clarifica Filium tuum, ut et Filius tuus clarificet te (Joan. XVII, 1). Par potestas. Sed sufficiunt ista de aequalitate Filii cum Patre.

Testimonia de Filii deitate.

7. In Job: Qui extendit coelum solus, et ambulat super mare tanquam super terram (Job IX, 8). In Jeremia: Hic Deus noster, et non deputabitur alius absque eo; qui invenit omnem viam prudentiae, et dedit eam Jacob puero suo, et Israel dilecto suo. Post haec in terris visus est, et cum hominibus conversatus est (Baruch III, 36, 37, 38). Nunquid quia hic persona Filii expressa est, dicendo, Quia non deputabitur alius absque eo, Patrem a deitate separamus? In Isaia: Fatigata est Aegyptus, et negotiatio Aethiopiae. Multi ad te venient, et tui erunt servi; et ambulabunt post te, alligati compedibus; et adorabunt te, et te deprecabuntur: quoniam in te est Deus, et tu es Deus solus, et nesciebamus: Deus Israel, Salvator noster (Isa. XLV, 14, 15). In hoc clarissimo testimonio, non solum deitas Filii, sed et summa cum Patre ostenditur aequalitas. Nam quod ait, In te est Deus, et tu es Deus, hoc in Evangelio dictum est, Ego in Patre, et Pater in me est (Joan. XIV, 11). Ad Romanos: Quorum patres, et ex quibus Christus, qui est super omnia Deus benedictus in saecula (Rom. IX, 5). Propria deitas Filii. Ad Corinthios secunda: Qui est imago invisibilis Dei (II Cor. IV, 4). Si imago, veritas. Ubi supra: Deus erat in Christo, mundum reconcilians sibi (II Cor. V, 19). Si Deus totus, non ex parte. Ad Ephesios: Evangelizare incomprehensibiles divitias Christi (Ephes. III, 8). Nunquid Christi solius, et non Patris? Ad Colossenses: Quia in ipso complacuit habitare

omnem plenitudinem divinitatis corporaliter (Coloss. II, 9). Hic adverte quia et omnem plenitudinem et divinitatem: ubi nihil est quod addatur. Ubi supra: Ut ostenderet Deus divitias sacramenti sui inter gentes: quod est Christus (Coloss. I, 27). Ecce, divitiae Dei Christus est. Ubi supra: Ut in agnitione sacramenti Dei, quod est Christus: in quo sunt omnes thesauri sapientiae et scientiae absconditi (Coloss. II, 3). Integra plenitudo. Ad Philippenses: Qui cum in forma Dei esset constitutus (Philip. II, 6). Audis formam, et negas aequalem? Ubi supra: Ipse autem Deus Pater, et Dominus noster Jesus Christus dirigat viam nostram ad vos (I Thess. III, 11). Ecce ambo dirigunt: par potestas. Ad Timotheum prima: Ut serves mandatum irreprehensibile, usque ad adventum Domini nostri Jesu Christi, quem suis temporibus ostendet beatus, et solus potens (I Tim. VI, 14), etc. Nunquid quia dixit, Solus potens, excluditur Pater a potentia? Ad Titum: Illuxit autem omnibus hominibus gratia Dei, et Salvatoris nostri Jesu Christi (Tit. II, 11). Ubi supra (v. 13): Exspectantes beatam spem et adventum gloriae magni Dei et Salvatoris nostri Jesu Christi. Si magnus Deus Filius, nihil habet minus. Ubi supra: Cum autem benignitas et humanitas illuxit Salvatoris nostri Jesu Christi (Tit. III, 4). Hic nec humanitatem tacuit, nec divinitatem. Joannes ad Parthos: Ut credamus in vero Filio ejus Jesu Christo. Hic est verus Deus, et vita aeterna (I Joan. V, 20). In hoc testimonio qui negat Filio perfectionem Dei, Antichristus est. Petri secunda: Sic enim abundanter ministrabitur vobis introitus in aeternum regnum Domini nostri et Salvatoris Jesu Christi (II Pet. I, 11). Et quamvis haec pauca testimonia de deitate Filii, quasi de magno mari ipsarum Scripturarum stilla elevata sit: cum omnis Scriptura tam ejus deitati quam etiam ejus pro assumpta carne humanitati perhibeat testimonium, sicut ipse in Evangelio secundum Joannem ait: Scrutamini Scripturas, quia vos putatis in ipsis vitam aeternam habere: et illae sunt quae testimonium perhibent de me (Joan. V, 39). Non ait, De nobis, ne duos introduceret deos. In Luca dixit ad eos Jesus: Haec sunt verba quae locutus sum vobis, cum adhuc essem vobiscum: quoniam necesse est impleri omnia quae scripta sunt in lege Moysi, et prophetis, et Psalmis, de me (Luc. XXIV, 44). Nunquid excludit Patrem a testimonio Scripturarum, quia et hic ait, De me? De omnipotentia Filii in Salomone: Omnipotens sermo tuus, Domine; de coelis a regalibus sedibus venit (Sap. XVIII, 15). In Zacharia: O, fugite de terra aquilonis, dicit Dominus: eo quod ex quatuor ventis coeli colligam vos. Dicit Dominus: In Sion salvamini qui habitatis in filia Babylonis. Propter quod haec dicit Dominus omnipotens: Post gloriam misit me ad gentes quae vos exspoliaverunt. Propter quod qui tangit vos, tanquam qui tangit pupillam oculi ejus. Propter quod inducam manum meam super eos, et erunt praeda praedantibus eos; et scietis quia Dominus omnipotens misit me (Zach. II, 2 et seq.). Sursum omnipotens dicit, deorsum omnipotens mittit: nunquid duo omnipotentes? Amos propheta: Dominus qui tangit terram et movet eam, et lugebunt omnes commorantes in ea; et ascendet sicut fluvius Aegypti, qui aedificat super coelum ascensionem suam, et remissionem suam super terram confirmat: qui vocat aquas maris, et effundit eas super faciem terrae: Dominus omnipotens est nomen ejus (Amos IX, 5). Nonne haec omnia Filio intelliguntur convenire? qui descendens terram tetigit, passione commovit, et de terris ascendit in coelum, et super terram descendit e coelo, sicut ipse promisit in Apocalypsi (Cap. III, 14): Haec dicit qui est testis fidelis, initium creaturae Dei: Qui est, et qui erat, et qui venturus est, Dominus omnipotens (Apoc. I, 8). Movet, quia dixit, Initium creaturae Dei; moveat, quia dictum est, Dominus omnipotens: ut hoc, de deitate; illud, quod natus est, de Maria Virgine.

Testimonia de Trinitate.

8. In Evangelio: Ite, baptizate gentes in nomine Patris, et Filii, et Spiritus sancti (Matth. XXVIII, 19). In nomine, non In nominibus. Item: Simile est regnum coelorum mulieri quae abscondit fermentum in farinae satis tribus, donec fermentaretur totum (Matth. XIII, 33). Hic mulier ponitur Ecclesia, quae aequis ponderibus fidem Patris, et Filii, et Spiritus sancti in corda credentium abscondit. In Apocalypsi: Sanctus, sanctus, sanctus Dominus Deus Sabaoth (Apoc. IV, 8). Tertio audio sanctus, et unum Dominum Deum. Ubi supra: Et dixit mihi angelus: Haec verba vera Dei sunt. Et cecidi ante pedes ejus ut adorarem eum; et dixit mihi: Vide ne feceris; conservus tuus sum, et fratrum tuorum habentium testimonium Jesu, et spiritus prophetiae (Apoc. XIX, 9, 10). Quid tam luce clarius ad ostendendam Trinitatem, nisi verba vera Patris, testimonium Filii, donum prophetiae Spiritus sancti? In Psalmis: Apud te est fons vitae, et in lumine tuo videbimus lumen (Psal. XXXV, 10). Apud Deum Patrem fons vitae Christus; et quia lumen est in ipso, illuminator videtur Spiritus sanctus: quia qui Spiritum Christi non habet, hic non est ejus (Rom. VIII, 9). In psalmo LXVI, 8: Benedicat nos Deus, Deus noster, benedicat nos Deus, et metuant eum omnes fines terrae. Ter audio Deum, et unum praedicat metuendum. In Epistola Joannis: Tres sunt in coelo qui testimonium reddunt,

Pater, Verbum, et Spiritus: et tres unum sunt (I Joan. V, 7). Quid dicam de patriarcha Abraham? qui cum trium speciem virorum videret, unum in eis Deum cognovit, cum dicit: Dominator Domine (Gen. XVIII, 3). Corporali ministerio tribus exhibet humanitatis officium; ab uno tamen prolis suscepit beneficium, dum dicitur ei: Ad hoc tempus veniam, et erit Sarae filius (vers. 10). Non dixit veniemus, sed veniam: ne plebem deorum introducere videretur. Nam ut noveris Trinitatem simul habitare, simul immunditiam declinare, audi quid in Evangelio Dominus dicat: Qui me diligit diligetur a Patre meo, et ego diligam eum (Joan. XIV, 21); et, Veniemus, ego et Pater meus, et mansionem apud illum faciemus (v. 23). Ecce, Pater et Filius unam habitant mansionem. Quid Spiritus sanctus? Audi Apostolum dicentem: Templum Dei estis, et Spiritus Dei habitat in vobis (I Cor. III, 16). Ostensus est Pater, et Filius, et Spiritus sanctus simul habitare; ostendatur ipsa Trinitas simul immunditiam declinare. Apud Salomonem habes: Perversae autem cogitationes separant a Deo: hoc de Patre. Quoniam in malivolam animam non introibit Sapientia: hoc de Filio. Spiritus enim sanctus disciplinae effugiet fictum, et auferet se a cogitationibus quae sunt sine intellectu (Sap. I, 3, 4, 5): hoc de Spiritu sancto. Sed ut compendio intellectus, Scripturae sensum de natura Trinitatis uniter dicentem colligas, in Exodo item habes: Ego sum Deus Abraham, et Deus Isaac, et Deus Jacob (Exod. III, 6). In psalmo: Vivit Dominus, et benedictus Deus meus, et exaltetur Deus salutis meae (Psal. XVII, 47). Paulus: Idem Spiritus, idem Dominus, idem Deus (I Cor. XII, 4, 5, 6). Nunquid offendit catholicum sensum quia Spiritus prius nominatus est? Item si Dominum quaeras ipsam Trinitatem dictam, audi: Afferte Domino gloriam et honorem, afferte Domino gloriam nominis ejus (Psal. XXVIII, 2). Quia Rex ipsa Trinitas: Auferte portas, principes, vestras, et elevamini, portae aeternales, et introibit Rex gloriae. Quis est iste Rex gloriae? Dominus virtutum ipse est Rex gloriae (Psal. XXIII, 9). Testimonium datum, Deum tertio repetitum, Dominum tertio appellatum Regem. Nec dii, nec domini, nec reges distincti sunt, quia in trina nomina et personas discernuntur: nam una deitas, unum dominium, unum regale imperium. Qui huic veritati studio male vincendi contradicit, non dico damnabitur, sed jam damnatus est.

Testimonia de Spiritu sancto, quia Deus est.

9. In principio libri Genesis: Et Spiritus Dei ferebatur super aquas (Genes. I, 2): qui in figura baptismi aquas sanctificaret, non qui lassando pausaret. In Job: Spiritus divinus est qui fecit me, et Spiritus Omnipotentis qui docet me (Job XXXIII, 4). In divinitate perfectio. In Evangelio: Spiritus est Deus, et qui adorant eum, in spiritu et veritate oportet adorare (Joan. IV, 24). Item: Non enim ad mensuram dat Deus Spiritum (Joan. III, 31). Ecce Spiritus immensus est. Ad Nicodemum: Spiritus enim ubi vult spirat, et vocem ejus audis, et nescis unde veniat vel quo vadat (Ibid., 8). Quando audis, Ubi vult, propria potestas est. In seipso Christus: Spiritus Domini super me (Luc. IV, 18). Nisi pius revocet has voces intellectus, major erit Spiritus Filio. Item: Jesus repletus Spiritu sancto, reversus est ab Jordane (Ibid., 1). Similis intellectus. Item: Si ergo videritis Filium hominis ascendentem ubi erat prius. Spiritus est qui vivificat: nam caro non prodest quidquam (Joan. VI, 63). Nihil minus habet deitatis qui vivificat. Item: Cum venerit Paracletus, Spiritus veritatis, quem Pater mittet in nomine meo, ipse introducet vos in omnem veritatem, et docebit vos (Joan. XVI, 13). Deus est qui introducet in omnem veritatem. In Actibus apostolorum, Petrus Cornelio: Jesum a Nazareth, quem unxit Deus Spiritu sancto (Act. X, 38). Homo unctus est, non Deus. Item Ananiae: Quare tentavit Satanas cor tuum, mentiri te Spiritui sancto (Act. V, 3)? Et infert: Non es mentitus hominibus, sed Deo (vers. 4). Item: Haec dicit Spiritus sanctus: Segregate mihi Saulum et Barnabam, in ministerio quo vocari eos (Act. XIII, 2). Hic nec Patris nec Filii inducit personam, quos tamen sanus intellectus non separat a jussione. Item Apostolus gentibus per Epistolam: Placuit, inquit, Spiritui sancto, et nobis, non imponere vobis amplius quam ut abstineatis ab idolis, a fornicatione, et sanguine (Act. XV, 28). Nunquid haec jussio sine Patre et Filio facta est? Item ibi: Dixit autem Spiritus Petro: Exsurgens vade cum illis, quia ego eos misi ad te (Act. X, 19). Nunquid nisi creator imperat creaturae? Item ibi: A Mileto autem Paulus mittens Ephesum, convocavit presbyteros et majores natu (Act. XX, 17); et post multam exhortationem intulit: Attendite gregem Christi, in quo vos Spiritus sanctus constituit episcopos (Ibid., 28). Nunquid ab hac constitutione sacerdotis separatur Pater aut Filius? Paulus ad Romanos: Spiritus autem vita aeterna, et pax (Rom. VIII, 6). Hoc Pater, hoc Filius, hoc Spiritus sanctus; sed una vita, non tres. Ubi supra: Spiritus vita est propter justitiam (Ibid., 10). Hoc Pater, hoc Filius. Ubi supra: Si autem Spiritus

ejus, qui suscitavit Christum a mortuis, habitat in vobis (v. 11). Qualis hic est Deus qui carnem Creatoris a mortuis suscitavit? Ubi supra: Non enim accepimus spiritum servitutis (v. 15). Nullus liber nisi Deus, quod est Spiritus sanctus. Ubi supra: Deus autem spei repleat vos omni gaudio et pace in credendo: in abundantia spei et virtute Spiritus sancti (Rom. XV, 13). Sicut Christus virtus Dei ita Spiritus sanctus. Ubi supra: Ut fiat oblatio gentium sanctificata in Spiritu sancto (Ibid., 16). Spiritus sicut vivificat, ita et sanctificat. Ubi supra: Non enim audeo aliquid loqui eorum quae per me non efficit Christus in obedientiam gentium, verbo et factis; per potentiam signorum et prodigiorum, in virtute Spiritus sancti (Ibid., 18, 19). Virtus Filius, virtus Spiritus, virtus Pater; sed una, non tres. Ad Corinthios prima: Spiritus autem omnia scrutatur. Nemo novit quae sunt Dei, nisi Spiritus ejus (I Cor. II, 10, 11). Ubi supra: Templum Dei estis, et Spiritus Dei habitat in vobis (I Cor. III, 16). Deus est qui habitat in templo suo. Ubi supra: Abluti et sanctificati estis in nomine Domini nostri Jesu Christi, et Spiritu Dei nostri (I Cor. VI, 11). Ecce simul mundant, simul sanctificant Filius et Spiritus sanctus. Ubi supra: Omnia operatur unus atque idem Spiritus, dividens unicuique prout vult (I Cor. XII, 11). Qui libere quod vult facit, nulli est subditus. Ad Corinthios secunda: Epistola scripta, non atramento, sed Spiritu Dei vivi (II Cor. III, 3). Spiritus hominis non est minor homine; quanto magis Spiritus Dei! Ubi supra: Littera occidit, Spiritus autem vivificat (Ibid., 6). Qui vivificat Deus est: quia Dominus mortificat et vivificat (I Reg. II, 6). Ad Galatas: Ut benedictionem Spiritus accipiamus per fidem (Gal. III, 14). Deus est qui benedicit. Ubi supra: Spiritu vivimus, Spiritu et ambulemus (Gal. V, 25). Qui rursum benedicit, ipse vivificat ut Deus. Ubi supra: Qui seminaverit in Spiritu, de Spiritu metet vitam aeternam (Gal. VI, 8). In his tribus testimoniis ad Galatas, Spiritus et benedicit, et vivificat, et dat vitam aeternam. Ad Ephesios: In quo credentes signati estis in Spiritu sancto (Ephes. I, 13). Signamur in nomine Patris, et Filii, et Spiritus sancti. Ubi supra: In quo vos aedificamini in habitaculum Dei in Spiritu (Ephes. II, 22). Item: Revelatum est sanctis ejus apostolis in Spiritu, esse gentes cohaeredes (Ephes. III, 5). Omnia operatur unus atque idem Spiritus: haeredes facit. Ubi supra: Ut det vobis secundum divitias claritatis suae, virtutem corroborari per Spiritum suum (Ibid., 16). Non corroborat nisi Deus. Ubi supra: Solliciti servare unitatem Spiritus in vinculo pacis (Ephes. IV, 3). Pax Christus. Nunquid duae paces? Ubi supra: Et gladium Spiritus, qui est sermo Dei (Ephes. VI, 17). Sermo Dei Christus; Spiritus sanctus sermo Dei. Nunquid duo sermones? Ad Philippenses: Sive absens audiam de vobis, quia statis in uno

Spiritu (Philip. I, 27), hoc est in Deo. Ad Thessalonicenses: Assumpsit vos Deus ab initio ad salutem in sanctificatione Spiritus (II Thess. II, 12). Ad Timotheum prima: Magnum est pietatis sacramentum, quod manifestatum est in carne, justificatum est in Spiritu (I Tim. III, 16). Ecce etiam Christi incarnationem Spiritus sanctus sanctificat. Ad Timotheum secunda: Bonum fidei commissum custodi, per Spiritum sanctum qui habitat in nobis (II Tim. I, 11) Si Deus non esset Spiritus, non auderet Apostolus per ipsum discipulum adjurare. Insuper, qui habitat in nobis. Ad Titum: Salvos nos fecit per lavacrum regenerationis, per Spiritum sanctum (Tit. III, 5). Petri ad gentes: Nuntiata vobis sunt per eos qui evangelizaverunt vobis, Spiritu sancto misso de coelis: in quo concupiscunt angeli prospicere (I Petr. I, 12). Deus est quem cupiunt angeli prospicere. Ubi supra: Christus pro peccatis nostris mortuus est, justus pro injustis: ut nos offerret Deo, mortificatos quidem carne, vivificatos autem Spiritu (I Petr. III, 18). Ubi supra: Ut judicentur quidem secundum hominem in carne, vivant autem secundum Deum in Spiritu (I Petr. IV, 6). Ubi supra: Si exprobramini in Christo, quoniam gloriae Domini Spiritus in vobis requiescit (Ibid., 14). Gloria Patris Christus est, gloria Spiritus sanctus. Nunquid duae gloriae? Petri secunda: Haec primum intelligentes, quod omnis prophetia Scripturae propria interpretatione non fit. Non enim voluntate humana allata est aliquando prophetia, sed Spiritu sancto acti locuti sunt homines Dei (II Petr. I, 0, 21). Nullus inspirat prophetiae donum nisi Deus. Joannis ad Parthos: In hoc scimus quia manet in nobis, de Spiritu sancto quem dedit nobis (I Joan. III, 24). Ubi supra: Quoniam in eo manemus, et ipse in nobis; quia de Spiritu suo dedit nobis (I Joan. IV, 13). Dedit, quod audis, operatio est virtutis, non separatio deitatis. In Apocalypsi: Et post dies tres et dimidium, Spiritus vitae a Deo intravit in eos; et steterunt super pedes suos (Apoc. XI, 11). Quod a Deo procedit, Deus est. Ubi supra: Scribe, Beati mortui qui in Domino moriuntur. Amodo jam dicit Spiritus ut requiescant a laboribus suis (Apoc. XIV, 13). Non dixit Pater, non dixit Filius, sed Spiritus, qui per hanc jussionem ostenditur Deus. Ad Hebraeos: Si enim sanguis taurorum et hircorum, et cinis vitulae aspersus, inquinatos sanctificat ad emundationem carnis, quanto magis sanguis Christi, qui per Spiritum sanctum seipsum obtulit immaculatum Deo (Hebr. IX, 13, 14)! Hoc testimonium docet cujus potestatis sit Spiritus sanctus, per quem caro Christi exhibetur immaculata. Ubi supra: Irritam quis faciens legem Moysi, sine ulla miseratione, duobus vel tribus testibus moritur: quanto magis putatis deteriora mereri supplicia qui Filium Dei conculcaverit, et sanguinem Testamenti pollutum duxerit, et Spiritui gratiae contumeliam fecerit (Hebr. X,

28, 29)! Ecce qualis ultio pro injuria Filii et Spiritus sancti. Ubi supra: Judicem omnium Deum, et Spiritus justorum perfectorum, et Testamenti Novi mediatorem Jesum Christum (Hebr. XII, 23). Hoc testimonium convenit Trinitati, quia et Pater, et Filius, et Spiritus sanctus hic nominatus est. Quia omnipotens est Spiritus sanctus, in Salomone: Spiritus sanctus, multiplex, subtilis, disertus, securus, incontaminatus, omnem habens virtutem (Sap. VII, 22). Et negas omnipotentem? Quia judex est Spiritus sanctus, dicit Dominus: Si abiero, mittam eum ad vos; et cum venerit, ipse arguet mundum de peccato, de justitia et de judicio (Joan. XVI, 7, 8). Vides judicem, qui etiam ipsum, si dicendum est, vindicat Salvatorem: et audet ei quisquam subtrahere deitatem? Et quid dicam amplius de deitate Spiritus sancti? quem pertimescit David dicens: Quo ibo, Domine, a Spiritu tuo, aut a facie tua quo fugiam (Psal. CXXXVIII, 7)? Et ut concludam, tantus ac talis est Spiritus sanctus, in quo si quis blasphemaverit, inveniet eum non sibi relaxantem, neque in isto saeculo, neque in futuro.

Fides catholica.

10. Ineffabilem illam Divinitatis substantiam vel naturam humanis verbis exprimere impossibile est: inconvertibilem, immutabilem, impassibilem, simplicem, incompositam, indivisibilem, inaccessam lucem, inexplicabilem virtutem, sine fine magnitudinem, gloriam inconspicabilem, bonitatem concupiscibilem, inexquisitum decorem, qui mentis quidem purae contingat et moveat affectum, indicari autem atque explicari non possit. Ubi est Pater, et Filius, et Spiritus sanctus, sola natura quae creata non est, dominationis potestas, bonitas naturalis. Pater initium omnium, causa cunctorum, radix viventium: a quo procedit fons vitae, virtus et imago indemutata invisibilis Dei, qui est Filius a Patre genitus. Verbum, sive ratio vivens; qui erat semper, et erat apud Deum, et Deus erat, non factus ex Patre ante saecula, non assumptus postmodum vel adoptatus in filium, non possessione vel factura, sed creator et factor omnium: qui est omnia quae Pater est; cui Pater omnia quae habet gignendo dedit. Et ubi ergo qui dedit, gignendo dedit; et qui accepit, nascendo accepit; non inopi subventum est, sed ipsa copia nata est. Non enim ille qui accepit, illi qui dedit potest esse inaequalis, quia et hoc nascendo accepit ut esset aequalis. Nihil enim Patre minus habet ille qui dixit: Omnia quae habet Pater mea sunt (Joan. XVI, 15). Et quia semetipsum exinanivit, formam servi

accipiens, non formam Dei perdens, in eadem forma servi factus est obediens usque ad mortem, mortem autem crucis; in qua paulo minus minoratus est ab angelis, ut in forma Dei maneret aequalis; quia non est forma illa mutabilis. Qui in coelo spiritibus mundis intellectualibus in forma Dei et Deo aequalis, ut Deus praebet exemplum; ut se idem exemplum redeunti etiam lapso praeberet homini, qui propter immunditiam peccatorum poenamque mortalitatis Deum videre non poterat: semetipsum exinanivit non amittendo divinitatem suam, sed assumendo humanitatem nostram: et formam servi accipiens, venit ad nos in hunc mundum, qui in hoc mundo erat, quia mundus per ipsum factus est (Joan. I, 10), ut exemplum sursum videntibus Deum, exemplum deorsum mirantibus hominem: exemplum sanis ad permanendum, exemplum infirmis ad convalescendum; exemplum morituris ad non timendum, exemplum mortuis ad resurgendum fieret: ipse in omnibus primatum tenens: ut quia homo ad beatitudinem sequi non debebat nisi Deum, et sentire non poterat Deum; sequendo Deum hominem factum, simul sequeretur et quem sentire poterat, et quem sequi debebat. Amemus ergo eum, et inhaereamus illi, caritate diffusa in cordibus nostris per Spiritum sanctum qui datus est nobis. Hic Spiritus et vita est, et vivificans lux, et illuminans; bonus, et bonitas; Spiritus rectus, Spiritus principalis, qui est Dominus omnium; mittens apostolos, separans sibi ministros, templa sibi ipse constituens, inspirans ubi vult, dividens donationes Spiritus prout vult. Spiritus adoptionis, Spiritus veritatis, Spiritus sapientiae et intellectus, scientiae, consilii, virtutis, et timoris Dei: per quem Pater agnoscitur, et Filius glorificatur. Neque enim dignum est, aut Filium aliquando defuisse Patri, aut Spiritum Filio: esset enim in maximis defraudata divinitas, et velut inglorium atque indignum duceretur, si velut ex poenitentia et praepostero consilio Deus ad perfectionis plenitudinem pervenisset. Qui potest capere capiat (Matth. XIX, 12): qui nondum potest, oret ut capiat, credat ut capiat: quia scriptum est: Nisi credideritis, non intelligetis (Isa. VII, 9, secundum LXX).

The Scriptorium Project is the work of a small group of lay people of various apostolic churches who are interested in the preservation, transmission, and translation of the works of the early and medieval church. Our efforts are to make the works of the church fathers accessible to anyone who might have an interest in Christian antiquities and the theological, philosophical, and moral writings that have become the bedrock of Western Civilization.

To-date, our releases have pulled from the Greek, Nordic, Visigothic, Slavic, Armenian, Syriac, Georgian, Anglo-Saxon, Byzantine, Persian, German, Celtic, Ethiopian, and Coptic traditions of Christianity, and have been pulled from sundry local traditions and languages.